Mother Teresa

The Story
of the Saint
of Calcutta

Written by Marlyn Evangelina Monge, FSP

Illustrations by Seung-bum Park

Pauline
BOOKS & MEDIA
Boston

Library of Congress Control Number: 2017955305

CIP data is available.

Originally published by Pauline Books & Media, Seoul, Korea. All rights reserved.

Illustrated by Park Seung-bum © Park Seung-bum

Written by Marlyn Evangelina Monge, FSP

Published by Pauline Books & Media, 50 Saint Pauls Avenue, Boston, MA 02130–3491

Printed in the U.S.A.

MTTP VSAUSAPEOILL9-1510097 4966-9

www.pauline.org

Pauline Books & Media is the publishing house of the Daughters of St. Paul, an international congregation of women religious serving the Church with the communications media.

1 2 3 4 5 6 7 8 9   22 21 20 19 18

Contents

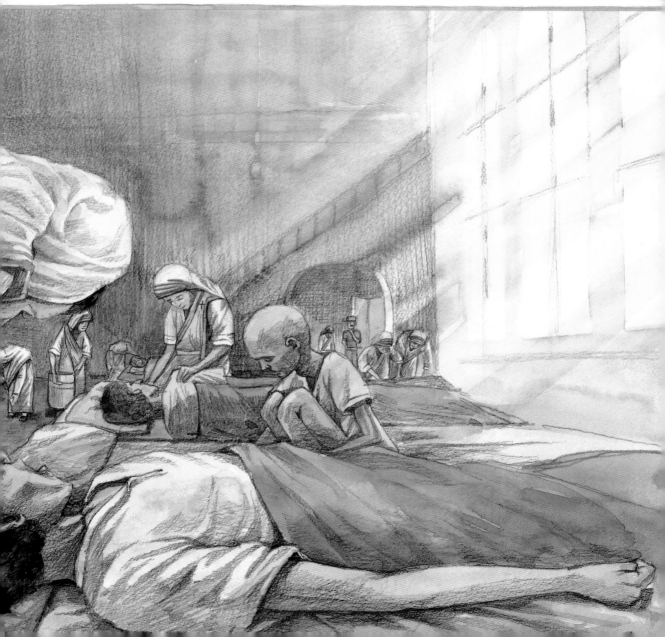

Little Rosebud

Skopje [SKO-pyeh], Yugoslavia, in 1915.

"Wash up quickly, children," Mama Drana [DRAH-nah] instructed. "Your father will be home soon." Twelve-year-old Aga [AH-guh] took her little sister, Agnes, by the hand to help her wash her face. Seven-year-old Lazar [LAH-zahr] followed. When they had finished washing, they heard the front door open and close.

"Where's my little Rosebud?" Nikola Bojaxhiu [NEE-ko-lah boy-ah-CHEW] called out.

"Papa!" Five-and-a-half-year-old Agnes laughed. Then she ran into her father's outstretched arms. "I'm right here!"

"Where are your brother and sister?" Papa Nikola asked.

"They're coming. We were playing a game in the parlor. Lazar was winning," the little girl said with a slight pout.

Papa Nikola smiled and patted her head. "I hope you were being a good sport," he said.

"I tried to be one. But I do like to win," the little girl replied. "Papa, you know what tomorrow is, right?"

"Tomorrow is Sunday," Papa Nikola said. "There is no council meeting, and my business will be closed. But I seem to recall that something special is happening. . . ." He tapped his daughter's nose.

"Don't you remember?" Agnes asked, her eyes opened widely. "I make my first Holy Communion tomorrow! I'm going to receive Jesus!"

"How could I forget something so important?" her father replied. "I just wanted to make sure *you* remembered!"

The next day, at the family's parish church, Sacred Heart of Jesus, Agnes received Jesus in the Eucharist for the first time.

After Mass, Agnes could not wait to speak with her mother. "I love Jesus so much! When I received him, I felt like he was telling me how much he loves me. I will always love him."

Heartbreak

"A nice carriage is pulling up!" Lazar reported.

"That must be your father," Mama Drana replied. "He's been away for so long on business. I didn't know when to expect him home." Mama Drana got up and smoothed her dress. Then she opened the door to greet her husband. But Papa Nikola was not standing outside. Instead there was a man she did not know.

"Hello, Madame," the man said. "I am the ambassador from Italy. I was with your husband in Ireland—"

"Where is my Nikola?" she asked.

Agnes, who was now eight years old, stood behind her mother. She listened to everything the man with the funny accent said.

"He's in the carriage. My driver will bring him in." The man paused. Holding his hat in his hands, he continued.

"I'm sorry to tell you this, Madame Bojaxhiu, but your husband became very sick during the conference. I brought him home in my carriage to keep him as comfortable as possible."

My papa! Agnes thought, tears filling her eyes. *I hope Mama can make him better.*

But Papa Nikola's health did not improve. Shortly after he was brought home, Papa Nikola was rushed to the local hospital.

Later, Mama Drana sat down with Aga, Lazar, and Agnes and gave them the tragic news. "Your papa was very sick. The doctors did all they could to help him. They operated on him, but . . ." She took a shaky breath and continued, "Children, your papa has died."

They all cried and hugged one another for a long time. Agnes could not believe her father was gone. "I'll miss Papa so much," she said.

"What will we do, Mama?" Aga asked.

"I'll miss your father too. But we must continue as best we can. We'll live and act as your papa would want," Mama Drana said. "And right now, that means praying together as we do every evening. Who will lead the Rosary tonight? We can pray it for your papa's soul and for others who have lost loved ones today."

Agnes dried her eyes. "I can lead us tonight," she offered. "In the name of the Father, and of the Son, and of the Holy Spirit. . . ."

Trust in God

Things were not easy for the Bojaxhiu family after Papa Nikola's death. His business partner took over the business. But he did not help to support the grieving family. Mama Drana did some sewing for the neighbors to make money. Teenage Aga helped by working too.

The family struggled in many ways. Still Mama Drana always shared what they had with those who were less fortunate. She often invited the poorer townspeople to join the family for dinner. Mama Drana taught her children to trust in God's Divine Providence. God would give them what they most needed. He would bless their generosity to others.

One day Agnes, now fourteen years old, walked to Sacred Heart Church after school.

"Agnes!" one of her friends called out. "Where are you going in such a hurry?"

"There's a meeting of the Children of Mary Sodality," she replied. "It's a group of girls our age. We learn more about living our faith. Today the priest is going to tell us more about missionary sisters and the work they are doing. Do you want to come?"

Father Jambrekovic, a Jesuit priest, had started the Children of Mary Sodality. He taught the girls how to know what God wanted for them and many other things. Recently the priest had been speaking about the interesting work that missionary priests, brothers, and sisters did all over the world.

Father Jambrekovic was helping young Agnes understand what God wanted her to do in life. Agnes had been thinking about becoming a religious sister since she was twelve years old. But she was not sure how her mother would react.

One night she told her mother that she wanted to become a missionary sister.

"Agnes, you are too young to make such a decision," Mama Drana said. "Besides, you have always been a sickly child. You've had a weak chest and horrible coughs since you were little."

"But I believe God is calling me to serve him," Agnes replied.

"There is more than one way to serve the Lord," her mother said. "You sing in the choir. You play the mandolin. You tutor your friends. Those are ways of serving God too!"

When Agnes tried to explain about her desire to be a sister, her mother stopped her. Mama Drana had made her decision. For now, Agnes would go to school. She would continue to pray to know God's will for her.

Sister Teresa

Agnes' desire to become a missionary sister did not go away. It grew stronger the more she prayed.

"Mama, may I speak with you?" seventeen-year-old Agnes asked one night. She told her mother that she still felt God calling her to be a religious sister.

Mama Drana listened and then went to her room. She stayed there for twenty-four hours! Agnes waited, wondered, and prayed. When Mama Drana came out, she went in search of her youngest daughter.

"It will be hard to let you go," Mama Drana told her. "But I give you my permission *and* my blessing."

"Thank you!" Agnes said as she hugged her mother.

"I want you to remember one thing," Mama Drana added. "You must always be devoted to God alone."

Agnes wanted to become a Loreto Sister and teach children about God. She was soon on a train bound for Paris, France. There she and another girl met with Mother Eugene MacAvin. The Loreto Sister interviewed both girls with the help of an interpreter. She recommended them to enter postulancy, the first step to becoming a religious sister. So they traveled to Rathfarnham, Dublin. This is where the motherhouse of the Loreto Sisters was located.

"You will stay here in Ireland for a few weeks to learn English," the two young women were told. "Then you will be sent to India for your novitiate. Novitiate is the second stage of preparation." They were on their way to becoming Loreto Sisters!

The two young women arrived in Calcutta by boat on January 6, 1929. A week later they went to the city of Darjeeling. There they continued their religious formation and learned more English.

On May 23, 1929, eighteen-year-old Agnes entered novitiate. As a novice, Agnes received the black habit and veil of the Loreto Sisters. She also received a new name. She was now Sister Mary Teresa of the Child Jesus. She picked this name to honor one of her favorite saints, Saint Thérèse of Lisieux.

For the next two years Sister Teresa studied to be a teacher. She learned more English as well as Hindi and Bengali—two common languages in India. Sister Teresa was very happy. On May 24, 1931, she made the vows of poverty, chastity, and obedience for the first time. She looked forward to carrying out whatever God asked of her.

Teacher and Friend

"Sister Teresa, where are you going?" asked a student at St. Mary's School. The school was in Entally, a neighborhood in Calcutta.

"Where I go every Sunday. I visit some of the families in the *bustees*," she replied.

"You're going to the slums? Why?" the girl asked.

"The people there have so little. I want to share what I have," explained Sister Teresa.

"But it's dangerous! And if you keep giving your things away, soon you won't have what you need," the girl reasoned.

"Don't worry about me. I'll be safe. And as for giving my things away, God always provides what I truly need." With that Sister Teresa smiled and walked away.

The girl was left thinking about her favorite instructor. Sister Teresa was a very popular teacher who had a kind word for everyone. She taught geography and history to the girls in the boarding school. She also taught them how important it was to care for those in need and to trust in God's Divine Providence. The girl hurried to her room. She wanted to see what she could give to Sister Teresa to share with the people in the *bustees*.

On May 14, 1937, Teresa vowed to live as a religious sister for the rest of her life. After this, as was the custom for all Loreto Sisters, she was referred to as Mother Teresa.

In the years that followed, Mother Teresa continued to teach the young women at Entally. For a while she also served as headmistress of the school. She always had a lot to do. Before long Mother Teresa's health began to suffer.

Inspiration Day

There was on-going violence between the Hindus and Muslims in Calcutta in 1946. This meant little to no food was delivered to the city. The sisters and the three hundred girls in their school were hungry. Mother Teresa would often go out alone in search of food. And God always provided for them.

Mother Teresa loved teaching her students. But her health had never been good. She worked long days, and they didn't have much to eat. This left her physically weak. Her sisters were worried that Mother Teresa would get very sick. Father Van Exem, her spiritual director, was also concerned.

Her superior told Mother Teresa one day, "We are sending you to Darjeeling. You can rest and regain your health there. You will also be spiritually renewed during your annual retreat."

On September 10, 1946, Mother Teresa boarded the train for the long trip. It was over 380 miles to the foothills of the Himalayas, the world's largest mountain range. During that journey, Mother Teresa experienced something that changed her life.

God made her understand that he wanted her to leave the Loreto Sisters. God wanted her to work and live among the poorest of the poor. Mother Teresa came to understand what Jesus meant when he said, while dying on the cross, "I thirst." God revealed to her that Jesus thirsts for love and for souls.

Mother Teresa said nothing about her train ride during her retreat. Instead she spent a lot of time in prayer. She wrote her reflections on small pieces of paper.

In October, Mother Teresa returned to Entally. Shortly after, she met with her spiritual director. "I need your advice, Father Van Exem," she said. She told him about the train ride and the message from God. Then she gave him all the little pieces of paper she had written.

Father Van Exem waited until he was alone to look them over. He read that God wanted her to start a new order of sisters. They would be devoted to loving care of the poorest of the poor.

Lord, is this really what you want? Father Van Exem prayed.

Thanks Be to God!

"How are you today, Mother Teresa?" Father Van Exem asked.

"I'm well, thank you," she replied smiling. "It's been almost two years since that train ride to Darjeeling. Is there any news yet?"

"You've been very patient," he said. "You've also done everything Archbishop Périer [PAY-ree-ay] asked you to do during this time."

Mother Teresa looked at her spiritual director. Then, bowing her head she said, "I only want to do God's will. If God wants me to wait longer before beginning the work he is asking me to do . . . then I wait happily."

"The wait is almost over," the priest responded. "The archbishop received a letter from Rome. You have permission to leave the Loreto Sisters and start your work."

"*Deo gratias*," Mother Teresa murmured. With a big smile, she echoed the prayer louder. "Thanks be to God!"

"Since I asked you to not tell anyone, your sisters have no idea that you'll be leaving. Please tell them now," Father Van Exem instructed. After Mother Teresa nodded, he continued, "You will no longer be a Loreto Sister. But you are still bound by your vows of poverty, chastity, and obedience. Your superior will now be the archbishop."

"May I go to serve the poor now?" she asked.

"The archbishop would like you to give the sisters time to hear and accept this decision," he said.

The Loreto Sisters were informed on August 8, 1948, of Mother Teresa's upcoming departure. Many were sad that their sister was leaving. The following week Mother Teresa prepared to leave. She didn't just want to serve the poor of Calcutta; she wanted to live like a poor woman of India. For this reason, she purchased three *saris*. A *sari* is a type of wrap-around dress most Indian women wear. Hers were white and edged with blue stripes. This simple garment would become her new habit.

She showed the *saris* to Father Van Exem. She explained her reason for buying them. "These are made of the cheapest fabric. And I liked the blue—it is the color for our Blessed Mother." With that, Father Van Exem blessed her new habits.

The archbishop asked Mother Teresa to learn more about caring for the sick and dying before she began her work in Calcutta. She agreed to spend time with the Medical Mission Sisters in Patna, a city in northern India. On August 16, she took off her black habit and veil and put on her simple *sari*. With only a small bag, five *rupees* (worth about one US dollar at the time), and her train ticket, Mother Teresa quietly left the Loreto convent at night to catch the train.

Five rupees isn't much, Lord, she prayed. *I trust in your Divine Providence. Bless my dear Loreto Sisters, Lord. I will miss them so much. But I give myself totally to you and to whatever you want me to do. I am even giving up this place I have called home for so many years.*

Fast Learner

Father Van Exem walked around the hospital. He had gone to see how Mother Teresa was doing. Sister Stephanie of the Medical Mission Sisters showed him some of the things that Mother Teresa had learned.

"Mother Teresa has been with you for a few weeks," he said. "She insists that she has learned everything she needs to know. She says she's ready to begin her work. But the archbishop and I thought that she would be with you for at least six months or even a year." Father Van Exem looked around. He noticed that Mother Teresa was not with them. "By the way, where is she? I'd like her to join us."

Then Father Van Exem heard a familiar laugh. "I'm right here!" said the small woman in a white and blue *sari* standing close to them. Father Van Exem could not believe that he had not recognized Mother Teresa. He had known her for so many years, but he was not used to seeing her in the new habit.

He received another surprise. Sister Stephanie agreed with Mother Teresa! "She has learned how to care for the people she will meet in the *bustees*. Besides, I am sure that soon there will be doctors and nurses who will help her."

Satisfied, Father Van Exem returned to Calcutta. He found a place for Mother Teresa with the Little Sisters of the Poor. She would stay there until another place could be found.

In December 1948, she made her annual spiritual retreat. Then Mother Teresa began to work in the *bustees*. Every day she walked to Mass in the morning. Then she

traveled to the *bustee* she used to see from the Loreto convent. There she taught in the open-air school she started. It was just an outdoor space among the huts. Her eager students squatted in the dirt. Using a stick to write the letters in the mud, Mother Teresa taught her pupils the Bengali alphabet.

Before long her twenty students doubled and then tripled in number. She taught them hygiene, the alphabet, and gave them some religious instruction. She even awarded her pupils with bars of soap for correct answers! In the afternoon, Mother Teresa visited the sick and dying. She cared for their needs as best she could. In the evening, she returned home. She was always tired but overjoyed to serve the poorest of the poor.

Divine Providence

"A handshake will serve as our agreement, Mother Teresa," said the man extending his hand.

"God bless you, sir," she said. Mother Teresa was so happy! She had just rented two huts for five *rupees* each. "One hut will be a school. The other will be a place for the sick and dying that have no place to go," she told the man.

Later that night, she prayed in her room. *Thank you for helping me find the huts, Jesus. Bless the gentleman who rented them to us.* She looked at the cross on her wall, then closed her eyes again. *I also thank you for the teacher from St. Mary's who comes to help me. But there are so many people who need help, Lord. I trust that, in your Divine Providence, you will send more people to join me.*

Mother Teresa's days were very full, and she was at peace serving the poor. But those first few months were difficult. She begged door to door asking for money and materials to teach the poor children or care for the sick. Some people were happy to help. Many others refused.

For almost twenty years at the Loreto convent, Mother Teresa had shared her life with a community of sisters. Now she was alone, and at times she felt lonely. She was sometimes tempted to return to the Loreto convent. When these times came, she quickly turned to God in prayer. She prayed for courage and for others to help her.

Before any women could join her, Mother Teresa needed to find a place to live. One day, Father Van Exem came with good news. "A man named Alfred Gomes has agreed to let you use the top floor of a building that he and his brothers own. They said you can stay there for free!"

Once again God had provided for her. Mother Teresa moved into her new convent on February 28, 1949. She had very little furniture and was happy in her poverty. She used a box as her table and a bench as her book shelf. She had a green cabinet for an altar. Many nights she reminded God that now all was ready for other women to join her.

On March 19, 1949, a former student named Subhasini Das [Suh-BAH-shih-nee Dahs] was the first of many women the Lord called to join Mother Teresa. A little more than a month later, Magdalen Gomes also came to serve the poorest of the poor. Gradually the group grew. God's will for Mother Teresa and her companions had become a reality.

New Growth

The first ten women who joined Mother Teresa were all former students. Father Van Exem went regularly to teach them religion. They learned from him and from Mother Teresa how to love Christ in the poorest of the poor. They also did the work God asked them to do. They taught children. They cared for and comforted the sick and dying. And they begged for food or donations for the poor.

Mother Teresa and her companions were not yet officially approved as a religious order. In April of 1950, Archbishop Périer sent for Father Van Exem. When the priest arrived, the archbishop gave him an important task.

"Mother Teresa wrote some simple rules for her community," he said. "Father Van Exem, please write a polished version." These rules, called constitutions, were necessary for the Pope to approve the new order of sisters.

Father Van Exem began to work right away. With input from Mother Teresa, the constitutions were soon sent to Rome.

By the fall, Pope Pius XII gave formal approval to Mother Teresa's new order, the Missionaries of Charity. On October 7, 1950, Archbishop Périer celebrated Mass in the crowded convent chapel. That day Subhasini, Magdalen, and nine other women who had joined Mother Teresa became postulants in the new order.

The following April, the postulants became novices. Subhasini was now Sister Agnes and Magdalen was now Sister Gertrude. Mother Teresa was their guide and model. She taught them about the cheerful spirit God wanted them to have. The novices also learned that the work they did was to be balanced by a profound life of prayer.

Soon more women joined them. The space Alfred Gomes had given them was now too small. Mother Teresa and her postulants and novices prayed about this problem. They asked God to take care of their need.

Then one day, Mother Teresa and Sister Gertrude met Doctor Islam. Mother Teresa asked, "How much will you ask for your property?"

"How did you know I was thinking of selling?" he asked. "I haven't told anyone!" In the end, the doctor agreed to sell it for much less than he had planned to ask.

"Sisters," Mother Teresa told the others, "let us go to chapel and thank the Lord for this gift of a new home. May much good be done there."

A Typical Day

"*Benedicamus Domino.* . . . Let us bless the Lord,"
Mother Teresa called out at 4:40 a.m.

"*Deo gratias.* . . . Thanks be to God," replied the sleepy
postulants and novices. This is how they began their day,
Monday through Saturday. On Sundays they would rise
even earlier, at 4:15 a.m.

Once dressed, the young women headed downstairs
to the courtyard to wash their faces. They used ash from
the stove to clean their teeth. By 5:15 a.m. everyone was in
the chapel for morning prayer, meditation, and Mass. After
Mass, each sister ate five *chapatis*—a type of unleavened
bread—for breakfast. The *chapatis* had *ghee*, a kind of
butter, on them. They ate quickly, took a vitamin, and
drank milk.

Before leaving the convent at 7:45 a.m., each woman bathed and hand washed her clothes from the previous day. Then they went out to serve Christ by loving the poorest of the poor. They returned at noon for a simple lunch, rest, prayer, and classes with Mother Teresa. Afterward, they went back to serve the people in the streets. At six they returned home for an hour of prayer before the Blessed Sacrament. After a dinner of rice and vegetables, the women mended their torn clothing and had some time for recreation. At 10:00 p.m. they went to bed for a well-deserved rest.

The postulants and novices were happy to love and serve God in the poor. But their families did not always understand their daughters' vocations.

"My family won't talk to me, Mother," a postulant told her one day. "They are embarrassed to see me begging and taking care of people who are below our caste."

Mother Teresa listened with understanding. She knew that the Indian caste system of social classes was very strict. It was difficult for some Indians to socialize with people outside their caste. That was why the postulant had been rejected by her own family. This was even harder than being rejected by those who didn't know her!

"Tell God about this," Mother Teresa said. "Offer him your suffering for love of Jesus. But know that you are part of a bigger family—the family of humanity. This is why we care for all the poor, regardless of religion or caste."

Each Missionary of Charity owned very little: cotton *saris*, underwear made of rough material, a pair of sandals, a crucifix to pin on her *sari*, a rosary, an umbrella, a metal bucket for washing, and a thin straw mattress for sleeping. They were as poor as the people they cared for. Despite having so little, Mother Teresa and the sisters were happy to share in Jesus' poverty.

Dignity for the Dying

Each day the Missionaries of Charity went out on the streets of Calcutta to do whatever they could for the people dying of hunger or disease. Several doctors, nurses, and other volunteers helped the sisters. But there was no place to care for the poor. The city's hospitals had some rooms for those who could not afford medical treatment. But these rooms were only used for those who could be cured. Those who could not be cured had no place to go.

Mother Teresa went to a city official for help. "I understand why hospitals choose to give their beds to those who can be cured," she said. "But the dying deserve to be loved too. We will take them."

"Where will you take them?" he asked.

"We need a place where they can die with dignity," she

replied. "They will die knowing that they are loved. Can you find us a place?"

City officials were happy that the sisters wanted to help. In 1952, they gave the sisters a monthly sum of money to care for the dying. They also gave the sisters an empty building that had been used by Hindus traveling to the sacred temple next door.

Within twenty-four hours the sisters had cleaned the dusty rooms. Soon cots with dying people filled the rooms. All were welcome. Mother Teresa named the place *Nirmal Hriday* (NIHR-mahl HRIH-day) or pure heart. Mother Teresa had a special devotion to Mary's Immaculate Heart.

Daily, the sisters collected almost lifeless bodies from the sides of the roads. Sometimes they even used a wheelbarrow!

The people in *Nirmal Hriday* were treated with love and tenderness. It did not matter whether the person was Hindu, Muslim, or Christian. The sisters did not try to convert anyone to Catholicism. Instead, they made sure that each dying person received the appropriate rites for his or her religion.

Some of the local Hindus, however, were angry. They did not want Catholic sisters to use this space. They thought the sisters were trying to force Hindus to become Catholic. They protested the work the sisters were doing. One man even threatened to kill Mother Teresa!

One day a leader of the protest snuck into *Nirmal Hriday*. He wanted to force the Missionaries of Charity out. Once inside, he saw the sisters clean the patients' infected, maggot-filled wounds. He observed how the sisters patiently fed broth to those too weak to eat. Finally, he noticed how everyone's faith was respected. The man was moved with profound respect for what Mother Teresa was doing.

When he got outside, the other protesters wanted to know if he was ready to kick Mother Teresa out.

"I will evict the sisters on one condition," he declared. "When your own mothers and sisters come to take care of these men, women, and children, then we can tell these Catholics to leave." The Missionaries of Charity were allowed to continue their work.

The first group of novices made their first vows on April 12, 1953. That same day Mother Teresa took Archbishop Périer's place as the superior of the Missionaries of Charity.

A Home for Every Child

"In every child we meet, we are called to see the child Jesus," Mother Teresa reminded the newest group of novices. "We love Jesus when we love them. Remember: Jesus said that whatever we do for the least of our brothers and sisters, we do for him."

Whenever Mother Teresa saw a need, she and her sisters tried to help. From the beginning they taught children living with their families in the *bustees*. But there were also abandoned children living alone on the dangerous streets. They had no adults to care if they ate or had clean clothes to wear.

Mother Teresa knew that Jesus wanted her to care for these orphans. In September 1955, she opened *Nirmala Shishu Bhavna* (NEER-maa-lah SHI-shoo BAH-haav-nah), the first of many homes for unwanted and orphaned children.

Some abandoned children were found in garbage cans, drains, railway platforms, or by the side of the roads. All of them were lovingly cared for at *Nirmala Shishu Bhavna*. Most of these children were starving. Many suffered from mental or physical illness. Some were so sick that they died shortly afterward. Each one was treated as a precious child of God. Each one was loved.

Mother Teresa knew that some poor mothers were afraid that they would be unable to take care of their babies. Some felt that they should have an abortion. That would kill the unborn baby. Mother Teresa told these mothers to have the babies and then give the babies to her. She promised that the children would be well cared for and, if possible, adopted by loving parents.

All the children that lived at *Nirmala Shisha Bhavna* learned to read and write. They also learned a trade so they could earn a good living.

The work that Mother Teresa and her sisters were doing in Calcutta was needed in other cities and countries as well. Soon the Missionaries of Charity opened convents all over India. In July of 1965, Mother Teresa and five Missionaries of Charity went to Venezuela. There they opened the first of many convents outside of India. Jesus called Mother Teresa to serve the poorest of the poor. She did everything she could to answer it.

In the Name of the Poor

Many people noticed the excellent work that Mother Teresa did. In fact, many countries honored this humble woman. They gave her medals and prizes for helping the poor. She always used her acceptance speeches as an opportunity to make more people aware of the needs of the poor and forgotten.

December 10, 1979, was a cold Monday morning in Norway. Mother Teresa quickly made her way to the University of Oslo. When she arrived, she was led to a large room. It was filled with well-dressed people. Then a man wearing a dark suit approached the microphone. He said, "I call upon Mother Teresa to receive the Nobel Peace Prize."

Mother Teresa walked up the few steps. She received the medal and turned. Then she folded her hands in prayer as the men and women who had gathered applauded her. Everyone grew quiet as Mother Teresa began to speak.

"Let us thank God that we have gathered to talk about the joy of spreading peace. We give thanks that we recognize that the poor are our brothers and sisters." Mother Teresa went on. She told these people from all over the world how much Jesus loves us. She reminded them that Jesus asked us to love one another just as he loves us.

"I am happy to receive this award in the name of those who are hungry and those who are naked," she said. "I accept it in the name of the homeless and those who are sick or have any kind of disability. I receive it in the name of those who no one loves or cares about—those who some might call a burden to society."

When she finished speaking, the people again stood and applauded. Mother Teresa was such a small woman, but she was mighty. She used every opportunity to invite others to join her in caring for Jesus' brothers and sisters.

Rescue!

Boom!

"Mother, you cannot go," said the head of the Red Cross in Lebanon. "The bombing and gunfire never stop!"

"But there are young people trapped in the hospital. They need us," replied Mother Teresa. "They must be hungry and scared. The building has been bombed. It will soon fall on them."

One of the Red Cross workers tried to reason with her. "It's too dangerous to go there!" he said.

The Dar Al-Ajaza Al-Islamia Mental Hospital was in the middle of a war zone. The fighting between Israeli and Palestinian forces was intense. Many innocent people were caught in the middle. Pope John Paul II had asked Mother Teresa to try to help them.

"The fighting will stop," Mother Teresa said firmly. "We will rescue the young people during the cease-fire tomorrow."

The Red Cross worker was unconvinced. "*If* the fighting stops," he said, "you have our full support, Mother."

Mother Teresa handed the workers a list of supplies to collect. Then she went to the chapel. She unpacked a beautiful Easter candle she had brought with her. There was a beautiful image of the Blessed Mother and baby Jesus on it. Mother Teresa lit the candle at four that afternoon. Then she sat on a mat on the chapel floor.

Lord, Mother Teresa prayed, *please make it possible for us to help those forgotten young people. I trust that you will make the Palestinians and the Israelis stop fighting. I leave it in your hands.*

Mother Teresa finished praying an hour later. All was quiet. The fighting had stopped! She came out of the chapel and spoke to one of the sisters. "Call the Red Cross. Tell them to get everything ready. The Lord has granted our request."

Early the next morning, on August 14, 1982, Mother Teresa and the Red Cross workers traveled to the hospital in four trucks. The trucks flew white flags. This showed that they were on a peaceful mission. Both Israeli and Palestinian fighters watched as the elderly sister led the workers into the hospital.

Inside Mother Teresa found thirty-seven children and young people. They huddled together on the floor on soiled rubber mats. Most were unable to walk. All of them had mental disabilities. She gently assured each of them, "You'll be safe now. We're taking you home. God loves you very much."

Mother Teresa picked up one of the children. With the help of the remaining hospital staff and the Red Cross workers, she and all thirty-seven patients left the hospital. They drove immediately to one of the convents of the Missionaries of Charity in East Beirut. There the children and young people were cleaned, fed, and loved.

Loved by Millions

Throughout her life Mother Teresa did not have good health. Still, she did all she could to ease the suffering of others. She was happiest loving Jesus by loving the poor. She met often with the pope and world leaders. She asked them to support her mission. She flew all over the world to encourage her sisters. "So many years ago, God asked me to love and serve the poorest of the poor. He asks you to do the same. I pray that you will always remain faithful to his call."

In January 1997, Mother Teresa stepped down as superior of the Missionaries of Charity. Her frail health meant that she spent a lot of time in and out of hospitals. On September 5, 1997, Mother Teresa's weak and tired heart stopped beating.

Her body was taken to St. Thomas Church in Calcutta. There the people she loved came to pay their respects. She was there for a week as huge crowds offered prayers of gratitude.

Her funeral Mass was on September 13. A procession carried her simple coffin from the church through the streets of Calcutta, which were lined with almost a million

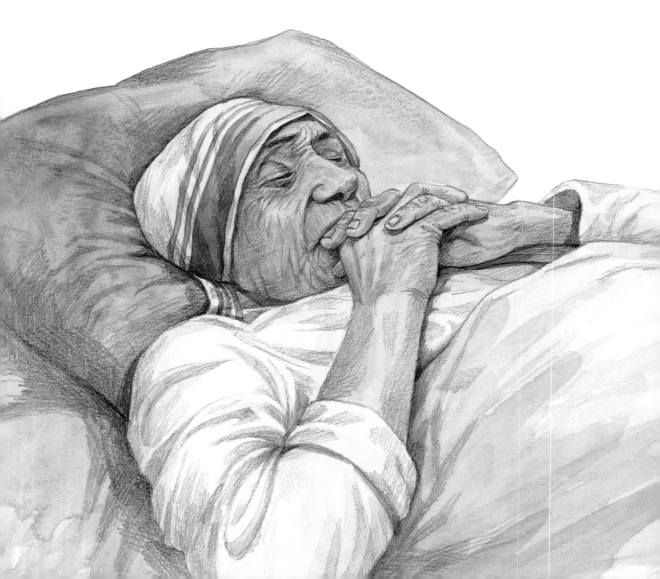

people. They threw flower petals to honor their mother. Many leaders and important people from around the world attended the funeral of this holy woman, who saw Christ in every person.

Six years later, Pope John Paul II proclaimed Mother Teresa "blessed." This means that the Church named Mother Teresa as a role model for the faithful. On September 4, 2016, she was canonized a saint by Pope Francis. Over 150,000 people crowded the plaza in front of St. Peter's Basilica in Rome to witness her canonization. Mother Teresa's call to love and serve the poorest of the poor continues today through the work of several Missionaries of Charity orders worldwide.

Prayer to Mother Teresa

Mother Teresa, you answered God's call to love him by serving the poorest of the poor. Because you saw Jesus in them, you spent your life loving the people we often ignore.

Pray that God will help me to see those who are in need.

Ask God to give me the grace to respond to their needs in love.

Guide me in doing what I can, where I am . . . one person at a time.

For, like you, I believe that whatever I do for the least of my brothers and sisters, I do for Jesus. Amen.

Awaken faith.
Inspire courage.
Communicate love.

Discover men and women who loved God and changed the world—and continue to inspire young hearts to follow in their footsteps—with more illustrated biographies from *Pauline*

Our Blessed Mother

The story of Mary's life and her role as Jesus' mother is presented in this beautifully illustrated book for children ages 7 to 9. The book also includes information about Mary's earthly apparitions, her feast days, and how to pray the Rosary.

ISBN: 0-8198-5504-9
$8.95 USD

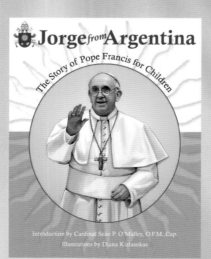

Jorge from Argentina

This delightfully illustrated biography for children ages 7 to 10 highlights the life of Pope Francis, the first pope to be a member of the Jesuit religious order, to come from Latin America, and to take the papal name in honor of Saint Francis of Assisi!

ISBN: 0-8198-4006-8
$10.95 USD

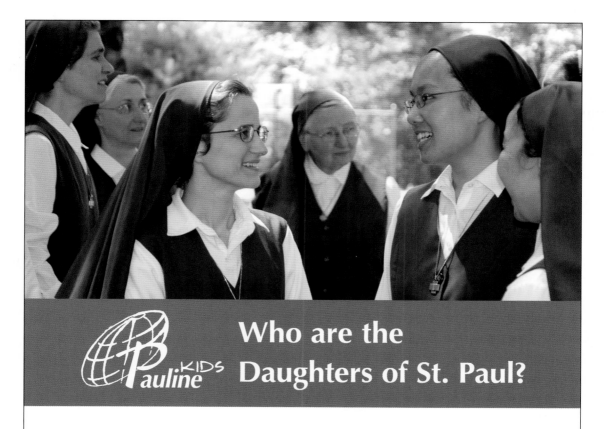

Who are the Daughters of St. Paul?

PaulineKIDS

We are Catholic sisters with a mission. Our task is to bring the love of Jesus to everyone like Saint Paul did. You can find us in over 50 countries. Our founder, Blessed James Alberione, showed us how to reach out to the world through the media. That's why we publish books, make movies and apps, record music, broadcast on radio, perform concerts, help people at our bookstores, visit parishes, host JClub book fairs, use social media and the Internet, and pray for all of you.

Pauline
BOOKS & MEDIA

The Daughters of St. Paul operate book and media centers at the following addresses. Visit, call, or write the one nearest you today, or find us at www.paulinestore.org.

CALIFORNIA
3908 Sepulveda Blvd, Culver City, CA 90230 — 310-397-8676
3250 Middlefield Road, Menlo Park, CA 94025 — 650-369-4230

FLORIDA
145 SW 107th Avenue, Miami, FL 33174 — 305-559-6715

HAWAII
1143 Bishop Street, Honolulu, HI 96813 — 808-521-2731

ILLINOIS
172 North Michigan Avenue, Chicago, IL 60601 — 312-346-4228

LOUISIANA
4403 Veterans Memorial Blvd, Metairie, LA 70006 — 504-887-7631

MASSACHUSETTS
885 Providence Hwy, Dedham, MA 02026 — 781-326-5385

MISSOURI
9804 Watson Road, St. Louis, MO 63126 — 314-965-3512

NEW YORK
115 E. 29th Street, New York City, NY 10016 — 212-754-1110

SOUTH CAROLINA
243 King Street, Charleston, SC 29401 — 843-577-0175

TEXAS
No book center; for parish exhibits or outreach evangelization, contact: 210-569-0500 or SanAntonio@paulinemedia.com or P.O. Box 761416, San Antonio, TX 78245

VIRGINIA
1025 King Street, Alexandria, VA 22314 — 703-549-3806

CANADA
3022 Dufferin Street, Toronto, ON M6B 3T5 — 416-781-9131

SMILE God loves you!